Flowering

Written by

Clare Mansfield

Illustrated by Cliodhna Murphy

Cover Illustration Faye Tucker

Once upon a time, there existed a beautiful flower called Daisy.

Daisy's favourite thing to do was to dance through the sun beams every morning.

Daisy was just a regular flower, nothing special, (or so she thought)...

... until the day she met Sonny, the Sunflower, who showed her how special she really was.

Sonny was strong and sturdy with a steady gaze, a beaming smile and a warm embrace.

Daisy and Sonny quickly fell in love.

She would giggle at his jokes and he loved to make her smile.

They loved to play together and they had lots of fun with their friends the birds and the bees.

They decided to stay together forever.

When they wanted to plant seeds to grow their own little flowers, they realised that Daisy had no seeds left.

She couldn't believe it. She was so sad. With every season and year that passed, she longed to grow life into their garden.

All around her were gardens full of bloom.

Even their grass looked greener.

Daisy soon stopped playing with the birds and the bees. She was too sad. She started to wilt as she looked at the emptiness around her.

Her friends, the birds and the bees, missed playing with her and worried as they noticed her wilting.

They called Doctor Stork, who was very clever.

Daisy took an immediate dislike to Doctor Stork.
He was very serious and he poked and prodded
her while asking her lots of nosey questions. He
infuriated her when he told her to relax and be
patient.

One day, they all teamed up; Daisy, Sonny, Doctor Stork, the birds and the bees, and they came up with a master plan.

There was a pretty young Posie who lived in a faraway field who heard of Daisy's plight and wanted to help.

She had lots of seeds and she generously wanted to share some with Daisy.

Posie already had her own beautiful garden and was upset to think of Daisy feeling so sad because hers was empty.

The birds and the bees then enjoyed playing a new game.

As Posie scattered her seeds about, the birds and the bees would catch them and carry them to Daisy. They had lots of fun scattering the seeds in the fresh soil around her.

Then they all played the waiting game. Daisy and Sonny practised patience. Throughout it all, the loyal couple stayed by each other's side. Their love kept them strong.

One magical day, a miracle happened. After 9 long months where they looked after the fertile soil giving it all the love, space, light, water, nurturing, shelter and encouragement it needed, not one but two seeds sprouted.

Daisy and Sonny were overjoyed! They both stood up tall and proud and shone brightly.

They named their beautiful, healthy little flowers Rosie and Poppy.

They all lived together in their colourful garden happily ever after.

This book is dedicated to my three little petals, Zoe, Lily and Isabella.

I would like to thank Ashley, Carolyn, Charlie, Dáire and Liam for all their help.

About the author

Clare Mansfield currently works as a Primary School Principal and Teacher. She is also a qualified Life Coach and a Holistic Therapist.

She is passionate about writing, teaching and helping others. Her first book *'Away with the Fairies - A Fairy's Guide to True Love'* was published by Seaburn Books in October 2013.

Her proudest achievement has been becoming a mum to her precious twin daughters Zoe and Lily and their sister Isabella. She is happily married to Shane and they all live together in Ireland.

www.floweringwithclare.com

About the illustrator

Cliodhna Murphy is a Primary Teacher from Kilkenny, Ireland who has travelled and taught in many countries around the world. She is currently living and teaching in Northern Italy with her husband Tom and they have welcomed their little boy, Tadhg into their family this year.

She has self published her two children's picturebooks, 'Fox Socks' and 'Berg the Narwhal'. Cliodhna is passionate about art, Gaeilge, and exploring nature.

Printed in Great Britain
by Amazon

29138787R00018